Linda

love
Deb

Fine Friends

Fine Friends

A Little Book About You and Me

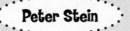
Peter Stein

**Andrews McMeel
Publishing, LLC**
Kansas City

For Lisa

07 08 09 10 11 SDB 10 9 8 7 6 5 4 3 2 1

ISBN-13: 978-0-7407-6310-6
ISBN-10: 0-7407-6310-5

Library of Congress Control Number: 2006932270

www.andrewsmcmeel.com

ATTENTION: SCHOOLS AND BUSINESSES
Andrews McMeel books are available at quantity discounts with bulk purchase for educational, business, or sales promotional use. For information, please write to: Special Sales Department, Andrews McMeel Publishing, LLC, 4520 Main Street, Kansas City, Missouri 64111.

Introduction

There's a fine art to being a fine friend. And like all great art, it's as completely individual as the artist. Yet there are certain universal threads that run through fine friendships . . . things like trust, a similar sense of humor, shared values, and—of course—a willingness to share the remote control.

To be a fine friend is to want the best for your pal. To grow together through time. To put up with the little faults, and even some of the big ones. (For the *huge* ones . . . please contact a professional. Pronto.) A fine friend will laugh with you, cry with you, sigh with you, and (when there's a good sale) buy with you. You can simply be yourself with a fine friend. And that's a rare thing.

How do you know when you have a fine friend? When someone tells you how wonderful you are, how you make their day, and that you have toilet paper stuck to your shoe. When someone can look you straight in the eye and say, "Chocolate," and immediately you know that means, "I need a shoulder to lean on." (Preferably with chocolate on it.) When someone knows you very, very well . . . and likes you anyway.

Being a fine friend is one of the best possible things you can do in your life. It's right up there with helping those in need, getting your back scratched, and watching old movies with a small truckload of popcorn. It simply makes you feel good.

Fine Friends is a celebration of all things friendship. Sometimes the very best thing you can do with a fine friend is to share a little "aha" moment . . . a small, knowing smile that says, "I may have toilet paper stuck to my shoe, but you, my fine friend, have food stuck in your teeth."

If you're holding this book, it's very likely you're a fine friend. And that is indeed a fine thing.

Fine Friends

A fine friend . . .

greets you warmly.

A fine friend . . .

wants only
the best for you.

A fine friend . . .

doesn't mind
staying in on a
Saturday night.

A fine friend . . .

brings out
the kid in you.

A fine friend . . .

will fetch a tasty snack for you.

A fine friend . . .

will drop
everything when
a big sale comes
around.

A fine friend . . .

often has similar tastes.

A fine friend . . .

enjoys practical jokes
now and then.

A fine friend . . .

will help you
remove a splinter.

A fine friend . . .

often calls to chat
about this and that.

A fine friend . . .

tells it like it is.

A fine friend . . .

doesn't mind engaging in a healthy debate now and then.

A fine friend . . .

misses you
when you're gone.

A fine friend . . .

often knows you
from way back when.

A fine friend . . .

will test you for
bad breath.

A fine friend . . .

can sometimes
be coaxed into
crashing just the
right party.

A fine friend . . .

can take you
to new heights.

A fine friend . . .

gently nudges you
when you need it.

A fine friend . . .

will sometimes
take you up
on a dare.

A fine friend . . .

pays attention.

A fine friend . . .

allows you to blow
off a little steam.

A fine friend . . .

doesn't abandon you during the tough times.

A fine friend . . .

always keeps
a secret.

A fine friend . . .

likes to gossip a bit now and then.

A fine friend . . .

doesn't avoid
you when you
wear the same
thing to a party.

A fine friend . . .

just might
inspire you to
dance, dance, dance!

A fine friend . . .

will tell you
if something's
stuck between
your teeth.

A fine friend . . .

**envisions
new horizons.**

A fine friend . . .

makes life
a little less scary.

A fine friend . . .

sees life much the same way as you.

I'm so glad . . .

we're fine friends.

Photo Credits